# The Perfect Air Fryer Cookbook

A Simplified Guide on How to Use Your Air Fryer

*Marta Cook*

# Table of Contents

# DESCRIPTION

First and foremost, the air fryer became popular for its numerous health benefits. The convenience and ease of use area close second and this combination make it an easy choice for those who want a healthy, delicious meal in a fraction of the time.

For those who doubt the air fryer capabilities and prefer conventional cooking methods, perhaps the following points will be enough to convince them to make the switch to efficient cooking.

An air fryer is made in way that there is a cooking chamber in which the actual cooking process takes place. Moreover, there is a drip tray placed into the air fryer basket, which allows you to cook crispy and tasty food.

An automated temperature controller in the air fryer plays an important role in determining how the final product will come out.

The digital screen and touchpad have made this device user-friendly because now users can control the device easily.

The buzzer will automatically inform you when the food is done.

This appliance comes with a manual for easy assembly and as a handy guide for first-time users. Most brands also include a pamphlet of recipes to give ideas about the wide range of dishes that you can create using this single kitchen appliance.

Once you are ready to cook and you have all your ingredients ready, put them in the basket and insert it into the fryer. Other recipes will require you to preheat the air fryer before using.

Once the basket is in, set the temperature and timer and begin cooking.

You can use an air fryer to cook food in a variety of ways. Once you get used with the basics, you can try its other features, such as advanced baking and using air fryer dehydrators.

In this book, you will learn more about:

- Breakfast
- Mains
- Sides
- Seafood
- Poultry
- Meat
- Eggs and Dairy
- Vegetables
- Snacks
- Dessert

...AND MORE!

# INTRODUCTION

Air fryers work by cooking food with the circulation of hot air. This is what makes the foods you put into it so crispy when they come out! Something called the "Maillard Effect" happens, which is a chemically induced reaction that occurs to the heat that makes it capable for this fryer to brown foods in such a short time, while keeping nutrients and flavor intact.

**The Benefits of Using an Air Fryer**

**A massive reduction in oil** –no more than a tsp or two of foil is needed to cook food in an air fryer and yet it still achieves the same texture. A far cry from the many cups of oil that you would have to use to cook food in a deep fryer. The result is food that is not soaked in unhealthy fat that will clog the arteries.

**Bursting with flavor** – the flavor of the food truly comes out in an air fryer. Despite the small amount of oil used in "frying" the food, the "fried" taste and texture is achieved.

**Easy press-and-go operation** –No longer do you need to watch over your frying pan on your stove while frying your food.

This also means no splattering of oil and accidental burns. All of the magic happens in the cooking chamber, just set your cooking preferences, push the right button, and let the air fryer do all of the work.

**Rapid cooking times** –The high temperatures that are circulated in the cooking chamber cut common cooking times in half. This is because the heat is maintained throughout the time being cooked meaning you do not have to worry about the loss of heat slowing down your cooking.

**Cleaning made Easy** –With food baskets that are dishwasher safe, it's as simple as removing it and putting it in. The cooking chamber can easily be cleaned with a cloth and a mild dishwashing soap.

**Versatile unmatched** – this modern appliance is more than just a fryer. You can bake, grill, and broil in it too. More of a highly versatile, mini convection oven rather than a fryer.

**Safe** – Its components are food safe and the cooking process itself helps you avoid kitchen accidents that can result in oil burns.

The body of the air fryer hardly gets hot even if the temperature inside is at its highest. Using your standard kitchen gloves will give you more than enough protection when handling this kitchen appliance.

These benefits make air fryers the obvious choice when it comes to healthy cooking No compromise on flavor or convenience!

To dumb it down, air fryers can do what those oil fryers do, but in a much healthier way than submerging food into greasy and fattening oil.

**Getting the Most Out of your Air Fryer**

To maximize the benefits of using an air fryer, here are some tips that you should not overlook:

**Getting Started**

- Place your air fryer on a level and heatproof kitchen top, if you have granite surfaces this is perfect.
- Avoid putting it close to the wall as this will dissipate the heat causing slower cooking times. Leave a space of at least five inches between the wall and the air fryer.
- Oven-safe baking sheets and cake pans may be used in the air fryer on the condition that they can fit inside easily and the door can close.
- Before Cooking
- If you can, always preheat your air fryer for 3 minutes before cooking. Once the timer goes off it will be ready to rock and roll.
- Use a hand pumped spray bottle for applying the oil. Adopting this method will cause you to use less oil and is an easier option when compared to brushing or drizzling. Avoid canned aerosol brands as they tend to have a lot of nasty chemicals
- Always Bread if necessary. This breading step should not be missed. Be sure to press the breading firmly onto the meat or vegetable so the crumbs do not fall off easily.
- Whilst Cooking
- Adding water to the air fryer drawer while cooking high-fat foods to will prevent excessive smoke and heat. Use this technique when cooking burgers, bacon, sausage and similar foods.

- Secure light foods such as bread slices with toothpicks so they don't get blown around.
- Avoid putting too many food items into the air fryer basket. Overcrowding will result in uneven cooking and will also prevent the food from getting that glorious crispy texture that we all love.
- Shaking the fryer and flipping the food halfway through the cooking process is advised to make sure that everything inside cooks evenly.
- Opening the air fryer a few times to check how the food is doing won't affect the cooking time, so don't worry.
- Once done:
- Remove the basket from the drawer before taking out the food to prevent the oil remaining on the food that you just fried.
- The juices in the air fryer drawer can be used to make delicious marinades and sauces. If you find it too greasy you can always reduce it in a saucepan to get rid of the excess liquid.
- Cleaning both the basket and drawer after every use is imperative.

Now that you've gotten to know the basics of using the air fryer, let's get to the exciting part — it's cooking time!

# BREAKFAST

## 1. Sausage Frittata

Preparation Time: 15 minutes

Cooking time: 11 minutes

Servings: 2

**Ingredients:**

- ½ of chorizo sausage, sliced
- ½ cup frozen corn
- 1 large potato, boiled, peeled and cubed
- 3 jumbo eggs
- 2 tablespoons feta cheese, crumbled
- 1 tablespoon olive oil
- Salt and black pepper, to taste

**Directions:**

1. Preheat the Air fryer to 355 o F and grease an Air Fryer pan.

2. Whisk together eggs with salt and black pepper in a bowl.

3. Heat olive oil in the Air Fryer pan and add sausage, corn and potato.

4. Cook for about 6 minutes and stir in the whisked eggs.

5. Top with cheese and cook for about 5 minutes.

6. Dish out and serve hot.

**Nutrition:**

Calories: 327, Fat: 20.2g, Carbohydrates: 23.3g, Sugar: 2.8g, Protein: 15.3g, Sodium: 316mg

## 2. Trout Frittata

Preparation Time: 15 minutes

Cooking time: 23 minutes

Servings: 4

**Ingredients:**

- 1 onion, sliced
- 6 eggs
- 2 hot-smoked trout fillets, chopped
- ¼ cup fresh dill, chopped
- 1 tomato, chopped
- 2 tablespoons olive oil
- ½ tablespoon horseradish sauce
- 2 tablespoons crème fraiche

**Directions:**

1. Preheat the Air fryer to 325 o F and grease a baking dish lightly.

2. Whisk together eggs with horseradish sauce and crème fraiche in a bowl.

3. Heat olive oil in a pan and add onions.

4. Sauté for about 3 minutes and transfer into a baking dish.

5. Stir in the whisked eggs, trout, tomato and dill.

6. Arrange the baking dish into an air fryer basket and cook for about 20 minutes.

7. Dish out and serve hot.

**Nutrition:**

Calories: 429, Fat: 38.1g, Carbohydrates: 5.5g, Sugar: 2.1g, Protein: 17.3g, Sodium: 252mg

## 3. Mushroom and Tomato Frittata

Preparation Time: 15 minutes

Cooking time: 14 minutes

Servings: 2

**Ingredients:**

- 1 bacon slice, chopped
- 6 cherry tomatoes, halved
- 6 fresh mushrooms, sliced
- 3 eggs
- ½ cup Parmesan cheese, grated
- 1 tablespoon olive oil
- Salt and black pepper, to taste

**Directions:**

1. Preheat the Air fryer to 390 o F and grease a baking dish lightly.

2. Mix together bacon, mushrooms, tomatoes, salt and black pepper in the baking dish.

3. Arrange the baking dish into the Air Fryer basket and cook for about 6 minutes.

4. Whisk together eggs in a small bowl and add cheese.

5. Mix well and pour over the bacon mixture.

6. Place the baking dish in the Air Fryer basket and cook for about 8 minutes.

7. Dish out and serve hot.

**Nutrition:**

Calories: 397, Fat: 26.2g, Carbohydrates: 23.3g, Sugar: 11.2g, Protein: 27.3g, Sodium: 693mg

## 4. Breakfast Zucchini

Preparation Time: 5 minutes

Cooking time: 35 minutes

Servings: 4

**Ingredients:**

- 4 zucchinis, diced into 1-inch pieces, drained
- 2 small bell pepper, chopped medium
- 2 small onion, chopped medium
- Cooking oil spray
- Pinch salt and black pepper

**Directions:**

1. Preheat the Air fryer to 350 o F and grease the Air fryer basket with cooking spray.

2. Season the zucchini with salt and black pepper and place in the Air fryer basket.

3. Select Roasting mode and cook for about 20 minutes, stirring occasionally.

4. Add onion and bell pepper and cook for 5 more minutes.

5. Remove from the Air fryer and mix well to serve warm.

**Nutrition:**

Calories: 146, Fat: 0.5g, Carbohydrates: 3.8g, Sugar: 5.5g, Protein: 4g, Sodium: 203mg

# MAIN

## 5. Fennel and Tomato Stew

Preparation Time: 25 minutes

Servings: 4

**Ingredients:**

- 2 fennel bulbs; shredded
- ½ cup chicken stock
- 1 red bell pepper; chopped.
- 2 garlic cloves; minced
- 2 cups tomatoes; cubed
- 2 tbsp. tomato puree
- 1 tsp. rosemary; dried
- 1 tsp. sweet paprika
- Salt and black pepper to taste.

**Directions:**

1. In a pan that fits your air fryer, mix all the ingredients, toss, introduce in the fryer and cook at 380°F for 15 minutes

2. Divide the stew into bowls.

**Nutrition: Calories: 184; Fat: 7g; Fiber: 2g; Carbs: 3g; Protein: 8g**

## 6. Courgettes Casserole

Preparation Time: 25 minutes

Servings: 4

**Ingredients:**

- 14 oz. cherry tomatoes; cubed
- • 2 spring onions; chopped.
- 3 garlic cloves; minced
- 2 courgettes; sliced
- 2 celery sticks; sliced
- 1 yellow bell pepper; chopped.
- ½ cup mozzarella; shredded
- 1 tbsp. thyme; dried
- 1 tbsp. olive oil
- 1 tsp. smoked paprika

**Directions:**

1. In a baking dish that fits your air fryer, mix all the ingredients except the cheese and toss.

2. Sprinkle the cheese on top, introduce the dish in your air fryer and cook at 380°F for 20 minutes. Divide between plates and serve for lunch

**Nutrition: Calories: 254; Fat: 12g; Fiber: 2g; Carbs: 4g; Protein: 11g**

# SIDES

## 7. Sweet Leek

Preparation Time: 10 minutes

Cooking time: 11 minutes

Servings: 2

**Ingredients:**

- ½ teaspoon baking soda
- 1 tablespoon sugar
- 11 oz leek
- 3 tablespoon cream
- ¼ teaspoon salt
- 1 tablespoon butter
- 3 tablespoon chicken stock
- ¼ teaspoon turmeric

**Directions:**

1. Chop the leek.

2. Preheat the air fryer to 390 F.

3. Toss the butter there and melt it.

4. Then add cream and chicken stock.

5. After this, add the chopped leek.

6. Sprinkle the leek with the sugar, salt, baking soda, and turmeric.

7. Stir it carefully.

8. Cook the leek for 5 minutes.

9. After this, shake the leek carefully and cook for 6 minutes more.

10. When the leek is soft and light brown – it is cooked.

11. Let it chill for 3 minutes.

12. Serve the meal.

**Nutrition: calories 182, fat 7.3, fiber 2.9, carbs 28.9, protein 2.6**

## 8. Soft Hasselback Potatoes

Preparation Time: 15 minutes

Cooking time: 30 minutes

Servings: 2

**Ingredients:**

- 2 medium potatoes
- 4 bacon slices
- ½ teaspoon salt
- ½ teaspoon ground black pepper
- ½ teaspoon ground paprika
- 1 teaspoon olive oil
- ½ teaspoon thyme
- ¼ teaspoon sage

**Directions:**

1. Wash the potatoes carefully but do not peel them.

2. Cut the slits in the potatoes to not cut them completely.

3. Place the sliced bacon into the potato slits.

4. Then sprinkle every Hasselback potato with the salt, ground black pepper, ground paprika, olive oil, thyme, and sage.

5. Preheat the air fryer to 400 F.

6. Put the Hasselback potatoes in the air fryer basket.

7. Cook the Hasselback potatoes for 30 minutes.

8. When the meal is cooked – chill it till the room temperature.

9. Serve it!

**Nutrition: calories 376, fat 18.5, fiber 5.6, carbs 34.9, protein 17.8**

## 9. Marinated Eggplants with Sesame Seeds

Preparation Time: 20 minutes

Cooking time: 12 minutes

Servings: 2

**Ingredients:**

- 2 eggplants
- 1 tablespoon sesame seeds
- 1 teaspoon canola oil
- 1 teaspoon apple cider vinegar
- ½ teaspoon chili flakes
- ¼ cup chicken stock
- 1 pinch salt
- ½ teaspoon lemon juice

**Directions:**

1. Peel the eggplants and cut them into the medium cubes.

2. Preheat the air fryer to 390 F.

3. Put the eggplants in the air fryer basket and sprinkle with the chicken stock salt.

4. Cook the eggplants for 8 minutes.

5. Shake the eggplants after 4 minutes of cooking.

6. Then drain the eggplants and transfer them to the bowl.

7. Sprinkle the vegetables with the sesame seeds, apple cider vinegar, chili flakes, salt, and lemon juice.

8. Mix the vegetables gently and put them in the fridge for at least 10 minutes to marinate.

9. Serve the cooked meal cold.

10. Enjoy!

**Nutrition: calories 186, fat 5.6, fiber 19.9, carbs 33.4, protein 6.3**

## 10. Air Fryer Mac

Preparation Time: 15 minutes

Cooking time: 5 minutes

Servings: 2

**Ingredients:**

- 6 oz mac, boiled
- 3 oz Cheddar cheese, shredded
- 2 oz Parmesan, shredded
- 1/3 cup half and half
- 1 teaspoon butter
- ½ teaspoon salt
- • ½ teaspoon dried oregano

**Directions:**

1. Toss the butter in the saucepan and melt it.

2. Add half and half.

3. Then sprinkle the liquid with the shredded Parmesan and Cheddar cheese.

4. Add salt and dried oregano.

5. Stir the mixture and simmer it on the medium heat for 3 minutes or till the cheese is melted and liquid is homogenous.

6. Preheat the air fryer to 360 F.

7. Put the cooked mac in the air fryer basket.

8. Add the melted cheese mixture and stir.

9. Cook the mac for 5 minutes.

10. When the mac is cooked – it will have the light brown crust.

11. Serve the meal immediately.

12. Enjoy!

**Nutrition: calories 578, fat 28.7, fiber 0.2, carbs 50.1, protein 30.6**

## 11. Roasted Cabbage

Preparation Time: 10 minutes

Cooking time: 7 minutes

Servings: 2

**Ingredients:**

- 12 oz white cabbage
- 1 tablespoon onion powder
- 1 teaspoon peanut butter
- ½ teaspoon olive oil
- 1 teaspoon oregano
- ½ tablespoon dried dill
- ¼ teaspoon ground black pepper

**Directions:**

1. Slice the cabbage into the thick wedges.

2. Rub the cabbage with the onion powder,

oregano, dried dill, and ground black pepper.

3. Then sprinkle the cabbage wedges with the olive oil.

4. Massage every cabbage wedge gently from each side.

5. Preheat the air fryer to 360 F.

6. Put the cabbage wedges in the air fryer basket.

7. Add the peanut butter and cook the meal for 4 minutes.

8. After this, flip the cabbage wedges to another side and cook for 3 minutes.

9. Then transfer the cooked meal to the serving plates.

10. Enjoy!

**Nutrition: calories 85, fat 2.8, fiber 5.1, carbs 14.3, protein 3.5**

## 12. Crunchy Broccoli Florets

Preparation Time: 15 minutes

Cooking time: 6 minutes

Servings: 2

**Ingredients:**

- 1 egg
- ¼ cup cream
- ½ teaspoon salt
- 2 tablespoon flour
- 1 teaspoon olive oil
- 12 oz broccoli

**Directions:**

1. Wash the broccoli and separate it into the medium florets.

2. Crack the egg into the bowl and whisk it.

3. Combine the egg with the cream and salt.

4. Stir the mixture.

5. After this, dip the broccoli florets in the cream mixture.

6. Then sprinkle every broccoli floret with the flour.

7. Preheat the air fryer to 400 F.

8. Put the broccoli florets in the air fryer tray.

9. Cook the broccoli for 5 minutes.

10. After this, shake the broccoli florets gently and cook them for 1 minute.

11. Then chill the broccoli gently and serve.

12. Enjoy!

**Nutrition: calories 157, fat 6.8, fiber 4.6, carbs 18.4, protein 8.6**

# SEAFOOD

## 13. Vermouth and Garlic Shrimp Skewers

Preparation Time: 15 minutes + marinating time

Servings: 4

**Nutrition: 371 Calories; 12.2g Fat; 30.4g Carbs; 29.5g Protein; 3.2g Sugars**

**Ingredients**

- 1 ½ pounds shrimp
- 1/4 cup vermouth
- 2 cloves garlic, crushed
- 1 teaspoon dry mango powder
- Kosher salt, to taste
- 1/4 teaspoon black pepper, freshly ground
- 2 tablespoons olive oil
- 4 tablespoons flour
- 8 skewers, soaked in water for 30 minutes
- 1 lemon, cut into wedges

**Directions**

1. Add the shrimp, vermouth, garlic, mango powder, salt, black pepper, and olive oil in a ceramic bowl; let it sit for 1 hour in your refrigerator.

2. Discard the marinade and toss the shrimp with flour. Thread on to skewers and transfer to the lightly greased cooking

basket.

3. Cook at 400 degrees F for 5 minutes, tossing halfway through. Serve with lemon wedges. Bon appétit!

## 14. Easy Lobster Tails

Preparation Time: 20 minutes

Servings: 5

**Nutrition: 422 Calories; 7.9g Fat; 49.9g Carbs; 35.4g Protein; 3.1g Sugars**

**Ingredients**

- 2 pounds fresh lobster tails, cleaned and halved, in shells
- 2 tablespoons butter, melted
- 1 teaspoon onion powder
- 1 teaspoon cayenne pepper
- Salt and ground black pepper, to taste
- 2 garlic cloves, minced
- 1 cup cornmeal
- 1 cup green olives

**Directions**

1. In a plastic closeable bag, thoroughly combine all ingredients; shake to combine well.

2. Transfer the coated lobster tails to the greased cooking basket.

3. Cook in the preheated Air Fryer at 390 degrees for 6 to 7 minutes, shaking the basket halfway through. Work in batches.

4. Serve with green olives and enjoy!

## 15. Spicy Curried King Prawns

Preparation Time: 10 minutes

Servings: 2

**Nutrition: 220 Calories; 9.7g Fat; 15.1g Carbs; 17.6g Protein; 2.2g Sugars**

**Ingredients**

- 12 king prawns, rinsed
- • 1 tablespoon coconut oil
- 1/2 teaspoon piri piri powder
- Salt and ground black pepper, to taste
- 1 teaspoon garlic paste
- 1 teaspoon onion powder
- 1/2 teaspoon cumin powder
- 1 teaspoon curry powder

**Directions**

1. In a mixing bowl, toss all ingredient until the prawns are well coated on all sides.

2. Cook in the preheated Air Fryer at 360 degrees F for 4 minutes. Shake the basket and cook for 4 minutes more.

3. Serve over hot rice if desired. Bon appétit!

## 16. Korean-Style Salmon Patties

Preparation Time: 15 minutes

Servings: 4

**Nutrition: 396 Calories; 20.1g Fat; 16.7g Carbs; 35.2g Protein; 3.1g Sugars**

**Ingredients**

- 1 pound salmon
- 1 egg
- 1 garlic clove, minced
- 2 green onions, minced
- 1/2 cup rolled oats

**Sauce:**

- 1 teaspoon rice wine
- 1 ½ tablespoons soy sauce
- 1 teaspoon honey
- A pinch of salt
- 1 teaspoon gochugaru, Korean red chili pepper flakes

**Directions**

1. Start by preheating your Air Fryer to 380 degrees F. Spritz the Air Fryer basket with

cooking oil.

2. Mix the salmon, egg, garlic, green onions, and rolled oats in a bowl; knead with your hands until everything is well incorporated.

3. Shape the mixture into equally sized patties. Transfer your patties to the Air Fryer basket.

4. Cook the fish patties for 10 minutes, turning them over halfway through.

5. Meanwhile, make the sauce by whisking all ingredients. Serve the warm fish patties with the sauce on the side.

## 17. English-Style Flounder Fillets

Preparation Time: 20 minutes

Servings: 2

**Nutrition: 432 Calories; 16.7g Fat; 29g Carbs; 38.4g Protein; 2.7g Sugars**

**Ingredients**

- 2 flounder fillets
- 1/4 cup all-purpose flour
- 1 egg
- 1/2 teaspoon Worcestershire sauce
- 1/2 cup bread crumbs
- 1/2 teaspoon lemon pepper
- 1/2 teaspoon coarse sea salt
- 1/4 teaspoon chili powder

**Directions**

1. Rinse and pat dry the flounder fillets.

2. Place the flour in a large pan.

3. Whisk the egg and Worcestershire sauce in a shallow bowl. In a separate bowl, mix the bread crumbs with the lemon pepper, salt, and chili powder.

4. Dredge the fillets in the flour, shaking off the excess. Then, dip them into the egg mixture. Lastly, coat the fish fillets with the breadcrumb mixture until they are coated on all sides.

5. Spritz with cooking spray and transfer to the Air Fryer basket. Cook at 390 degrees for 7 minutes.

6. Turn them over, spritz with cooking spray on the other side, and cook another 5 minutes. Bon appétit!

# POULTRY

## 18. Adobo Seasoned Chicken with Veggies

Preparation Time: 1 hour 30 minutes

Servings: 4

**Nutrition: 427 Calories; 15.3g Fat; 18.5g Carbs; 52.3g Protein; 9.4g Sugars**

**Ingredients**

- 2 pounds chicken wings, rinsed and patted dry
- 1 teaspoon coarse sea salt
- 1/4 teaspoon ground black pepper
- 1/2 teaspoon red pepper flakes, crushed
- 1 teaspoon ground cumin
- 1 teaspoon paprika
- 1 teaspoon granulated onion
- 1 teaspoon ground turmeric
- 2 tablespoons tomato powder
- 1 tablespoon dry Madeira wine
- 2 stalks celery, diced
- 2 cloves garlic, peeled but not chopped
- 1 large Spanish onion, diced

- 2 bell peppers, seeded and sliced
- 4 carrots, trimmed and halved
- 2 tablespoons olive oil

**Directions**

1. Toss all ingredients in a large bowl. Cover and let it sit for 1 hour in your refrigerator.

2. Add the chicken wings to a baking pan.

3. Roast the chicken wings in the preheated Air Fryer at 380 degrees F for 7 minutes.

4. Add the vegetables and cook an additional 15 minutes, shaking the basket once or twice. Serve warm.

## 19. Spice Lime Chicken

## Tenders

Preparation Time: 20 minutes

Servings: 6

**Nutrition: 422 Calories; 29.2g Fat; 6.1g Carbs; 32.9g Protein; 2.4g Sugars**

**Ingredients**

- 1 lime
- 2 pounds chicken tenderloins cut up
- 1 cup cornflakes, crushed
- 1/2 cup Parmesan cheese, grated
- 1 tablespoon olive oil
- Sea salt and ground black pepper, to taste
- 1 teaspoon cayenne pepper
- 1/3 teaspoon ground cumin
- 1 teaspoon chili powder
- 1 egg

**Directions**

1. Squeeze the lime juice all over the chicken.

2. Spritz the cooking basket with a nonstick cooking spray.

3. In a mixing bowl, thoroughly combine the cornflakes, Parmesan, olive oil, salt, black pepper, cayenne pepper, cumin, and chili powder.

4. In another shallow bowl, whisk the egg until well beaten. Dip the chicken tenders in the egg, then in cornflakes mixture.

5. Transfer the breaded chicken to the prepared cooking basket. Cook in the preheated Air Fryer at 380 degrees F for 12 minutes. Turn them over halfway through the cooking time. Work in batches. Serve immediately.

## 20. Quick and Easy Chicken Mole

Preparation Time: 35 minutes

Servings: 4

**Nutrition: 453 Calories; 17.5g Fat; 25.1g Carbs;**

**47.5g Protein; 12.9g Sugars**

**Ingredients**

- 8 chicken thighs, skinless, bone-in
- 1 tablespoon peanut oil
- Sea salt and ground black pepper, to taste

**Mole sauce:**

- 1 tablespoon peanut oil
- 1 onion, chopped
- 1 ounce dried negro chiles, stemmed, seeded, and chopped
- 2 garlic cloves, peeled and halved
- 2 large-sized fresh tomatoes, pureed
- 2 tablespoons raisins
- 1 ½ ounces bittersweet chocolate, chopped
- 1 teaspoon dried Mexican oregano
- 1/2 teaspoon ground cumin
- 1 teaspoon coriander seeds

- A pinch of ground cloves
- 4 strips orange peel
- 1/4 cup almonds, sliced and toasted

**Directions**

1. Start by preheating your Air Fryer to 380 degrees F. Toss the chicken thighs with the peanut oil, salt, and black pepper.

2. Cook in the preheated Air Fryer for 12 minutes; flip them and cook an additional 10 minutes; reserve.

3. To make the sauce, heat 1 tablespoon of peanut oil in a saucepan over medium-high heat. Now, sauté the onion, chiles and garlic until fragrant or about 2 minutes.

4. Next, stir in the tomatoes, raisins, chocolate, oregano, cumin, coriander seeds, and cloves. Let it simmer until the sauce has slightly thickened.

5. Add the reserved chicken to the baking pan; add the sauce and cook in the preheated Air Fryer at 360 degrees F for

10 minutes or until thoroughly warmed.

6. Serve garnished with orange peel and sliced almonds. Enjoy!

## 21. Chicken Sausage Frittata with Cheese

Preparation Time: 15 minutes

Servings: 2

**Nutrition: 475 Calories; 34.2g Fat; 5.3g Carbs; 36.2g Protein; 2.6g Sugars**

**Ingredients**

- 1 tablespoon olive oil
- 2 chicken sausages, sliced
- 4 eggs
- 1 garlic clove, minced
- 1/2 yellow onion, chopped
- Sea salt and ground black pepper, to taste
- 4 tablespoons Monterey-Jack cheese
- 1 tablespoon fresh parsley leaves, chopped

**Directions**

1. Grease the sides and bottom of a baking pan with olive oil.

2. Add the sausages and cook in the preheated Air Fryer at 360 degrees F for 4 to 5 minutes.

3. In a mixing dish, whisk the eggs with garlic and onion. Season with salt and black pepper.

4. Pour the mixture over sausages. Top with cheese. Cook in the preheated Air Fryer at 360 degrees F for another 6 minutes.

5. Serve immediately with fresh parsley leaves. Bon appétit!

# 22. Traditional Chicken Teriyaki

Preparation Time: 50 minutes

Servings: 4

**Nutrition: 362 Calories; 21.1g Fat; 4.4g Carbs;**

**36.6g Protein; 2.4g Sugars**

**Ingredients**

- 1 ½ pounds chicken breast, halved
- 1 tablespoon lemon juice
- 2 tablespoons Mirin
- 1/4 cup milk
- 2 tablespoons soy sauce
- 1 tablespoon olive oil
- 1 teaspoon ginger, peeled and grated
- 2 garlic cloves, minced
- 1/2 teaspoon salt
- 1/2 teaspoon ground black pepper
- 1 teaspoon cornstarch

**Directions**

1. In a large ceramic dish, place the chicken, lemon juice, Mirin, milk, soy sauce, olive oil, ginger, and garlic. Let it marinate for 30 minutes in your refrigerator.

2. Spritz the sides and bottom of the cooking basket with a nonstick cooking spray. Arrange the chicken in the cooking basket and cook at 370 degrees F for 10 minutes.

3. Turn over the chicken, baste with the reserved marinade and cook for 4 minutes longer. Taste for doneness, season with salt and pepper, and reserve.

4. Mix the cornstarch with 1 tablespoon of water. Add the marinade to the preheated skillet over medium heat; cook for 3 to 4 minutes. Now, stir in the cornstarch slurry and cook until the sauce thickens.

5. Spoon the sauce over the reserved chicken and serve immediately.

# MEAT

## 23. Pork Roast

Preparation Time: 35 minutes

Servings: 4

**Ingredients:**

- 1 lb. pork tenderloin, trimmed
- 2 tbsp. balsamic vinegar
- 3 tbsp. mustard
- 2 tbsp. olive oil
- A pinch of salt and black pepper

**Directions:**

1. Take a bowl and mix the pork tenderloin with the rest of the ingredients and rub well.

2. Put the roast in your air fryer's basket and cook at 380°F for 30 minutes. Slice the roast, divide between plates and serve.

**Nutrition: Calories: 274; Fat: 13g; Fiber: 4g; Carbs: 7g; Protein: 22**

## 24. Herbed Lamb

Preparation Time: 40 minutes

Servings: 4

**Ingredients:**

- 8 lamb cutlets
- ¼ cup mustard
- 2 garlic cloves; minced
- • 1 tbsp. oregano; chopped
- 1 tbsp. mint chopped.
- 1 tbsp. chives; chopped
- 1 tbsp. basil; chopped
- A drizzle of olive oil
- A pinch of salt and black pepper
-

**Directions:**

1. Take a bowl and mix the lamb with the rest of the ingredients and rub well.

2. Put the cutlets in your air fryer's basket and cook at 380°F for 15 minutes on each side

3. Divide between plates and serve with a side salad.

**Nutrition: Calories: 284; Fat: 13g; Fiber: 3g; Carbs: 6g; Protein: 14g**

## 25. Smoked Beef Burgers

Preparation Time: 20 minutes

Servings: 4

**Nutrition: 167 Calories; 5.5g Fat; 1.4g Carbs; 26.4g Protein; 0g Sugars; 0.4g Fiber**

**Ingredients**

- 1 ¼ pounds lean ground beef
- 1 tablespoon soy sauce
- 1 teaspoon Dijon mustard
- A few dashes of liquid smoke
- 1 teaspoon shallot powder
- 1 clove garlic, minced
- 1/2 teaspoon cumin powder
- 1/4 cup scallions, minced
- 1/3 teaspoon sea salt flakes
- 1/3 teaspoon freshly cracked mixed peppercorns
- 1 teaspoon celery seeds
- 1 teaspoon parsley flakes

**Directions**

1. Mix all of the above ingredients in a bowl; knead until everything is well incorporated.

2. Shape the mixture into four patties. Next, make a shallow dip in the center of each patty to prevent them puffing up during air-frying.

3. Spritz the patties on all sides using a non-stick cooking spray. Cook approximately 12 minutes at 360 degrees F.

4. Check for doneness – an instant read thermometer should read 160 degrees F. Bon appétit!

## 26. Spicy Holiday Roast Beef

Preparation Time: 50 minutes

Servings: 8

**Nutrition: 243 Calories; 10.6g Fat; 0.4g Carbs; 34.5g Protein; 0g Sugars; 0.4g Fiber**

**Ingredients**

- 2 pounds roast beef, at room temperature
- 2 tablespoons extra-virgin olive oil
- 1 teaspoon sea salt flakes
- 1 teaspoon black pepper, preferably freshly ground
- 1 teaspoon smoked paprika
- A few dashes of liquid smoke
- 2 jalapeño peppers, thinly sliced

**Directions**

1. Start by preheating the Air Fryer to 330 degrees F.

2. Then, pat the roast dry using kitchen towels. Rub with extra-virgin olive oil and all seasonings along with liquid smoke.

3. Roast for 30 minutes in the preheated Air Fryer; then, pause the machine and turn the roast over; roast for additional 15 minutes.

4. Check for doneness using a meat thermometer and serve sprinkled with sliced jalapeños. Bon appétit!

## 27. Rich Beef and Sausage Meatloaf

Preparation Time: 30 minutes

Servings: 4

**Nutrition: 206 Calories; 7.9g Fat; 15.9g Carbs; 17.6g Protein; 0.8g Sugars; 0.4g Fiber**

**Ingredients**

- 3/4 pound ground chuck
- 1/4 pound ground pork sausage
- 1 cup shallot, finely chopped
- 2 eggs, well beaten
- 3 tablespoons plain milk
- 1 tablespoon oyster sauce
- 1 teaspoon porcini mushrooms
- 1/2 teaspoon cumin powder
- 1 teaspoon garlic paste
- 1 tablespoon fresh parsley
- Seasoned salt and crushed red pepper flakes, to taste
- 1 cup parmesan cheese, grated

**Directions**

1. Simply place all ingredients in a large-sized mixing dish; mix until everything is thoroughly combined.

2. Press the meatloaf mixture into the Air Fryer baking dish; set your Air Fryer to cook at 360 degrees F for 25 minutes. Press the power button and cook until heated through.

3. Check for doneness and serve with your favorite wine!

## 28. Japanese Miso Steak

Preparation Time: 15 minutes + marinating time

Servings: 4

**Nutrition: 367 Calories; 15.1g Fat; 6.4g Carbs;**

**48.6g Protein; 3.4g Sugars; 0.3g Fiber**

### Ingredients

- 1 ¼ pounds flank steak
- 1 ½ tablespoons sake
- 1 tablespoon brown miso paste
- 2 garlic cloves, pressed
- 1 tablespoon olive oil

### Directions

1. Place all the ingredients in a sealable food bag; shake until completely coated and place in your refrigerator for at least 1 hour.

2. Then, spritz the steak with a non-stick cooking spray; make sure to coat on all sides. Place the steak in the Air Fryer baking pan.

3. Set your Air Fryer to cook at 400 degrees F. Roast for 12 minutes, flipping twice. Serve immediately.

## 29. Classic Keto Cheeseburgers

Preparation Time: 15 minutes

Servings: 4

**Nutrition: 271 Calories; 13.3g Fat; 21.9g Carbs; 15.3g Protein; 2.9g Sugars; 0.2g Fiber**

**Ingredients**

- 1 ½ pounds ground chuck
- 1 envelope onion soup mix
- Kosher salt and freshly ground black pepper, to taste
- 1 teaspoon paprika
- 4 slices Monterey-Jack cheese

**Directions**

1. In a mixing dish, thoroughly combine ground chuck, onion soup mix, salt, black pepper, and paprika.

2. Then, set your Air Fryer to cook at 385 degrees F. Shape the mixture into 4 patties. Air-fry them for 10 minutes.

3. Next step, place the slices of cheese on the top of the warm burgers. Air-fry for one minute more.

4. Serve with mustard and pickled salad of choice. Bon appétit!

## 30. Beef Steaks with Mediterranean Herbs

Preparation Time: 25 minutes

Servings: 4

**Nutrition: 445 Calories; 23.7g Fat; 11.3g Carbs; 51.1g Protein; 10.3g Sugars; 0.7g Fiber**

**Ingredients**

- 2 tablespoons soy sauce
- 3 heaping tablespoons fresh chives
- 2 tablespoons olive oil
- 3 tablespoons dry white wine
- 4 small-sized beef steaks
- 2 teaspoons smoked cayenne pepper
- 1/2 teaspoon dried basil
- 1/2 teaspoon dried rosemary
- 1 teaspoon freshly ground pepper
- 1 teaspoon sea salt, or more to taste

**Directions**

1. Firstly, coat the steaks with the cayenne pepper, black pepper, salt, basil, and rosemary.

2. Drizzle the steaks with olive oil, white wine, soy sauce, and honey.

3. Finally, roast in an Air Fryer basket for 20 minutes at 335 degrees F. Serve garnished with fresh chives. Bon appétit!

# EGGS AND DAIRY

## 31. Turkey with Cheese and Pasilla Peppers

Preparation Time: 30 minutes

Servings: 2

**Nutrition: 504 Calories; 37.8g Fat; 6.5g Carbs; 33.9g Protein; 0.4g Sugars; 1g Fiber**

**Ingredients**

- 1/2 cup Parmesan cheese, shredded
- 1/2 pound turkey breasts, cut into four pieces
- 1/3 cup mayonnaise
- 1 ½ tablespoons sour cream
- 1 dried Pasilla peppers
- 1 teaspoon onion salt
- 1/3 teaspoon mixed peppercorns, freshly cracked

**Directions**

1. In a shallow bowl, mix Parmesan cheese, onion salt, and the cracked mixed peppercorns together.

2. In a food processor, blitz the mayonnaise, along with the cream and dried Pasilla peppers until there are no lumps.

3. Coat the turkey breasts with this mixture, ensuring that all sides are covered.

4. Then, coat each piece of turkey in the Parmesan mixture. Now, preheat the Air Fryer to 365 degrees F; cook for 28 minutes until thoroughly cooked.

## 32. Baked Denver Omelet with Sausage

Preparation Time: 14 minutes

Servings: 5

**Nutrition: 323 Calories; 18.6g Fat; 2.7g Carbs; 34.1g Protein; 1.4g Sugars; 0.4g Fiber**

**Ingredients**

- 3 pork sausages, chopped
- 8 well-beaten eggs
- 1 ½ bell peppers, seeded and chopped
- 1 teaspoon smoked cayenne pepper
- 2 tablespoons Fontina cheese
- 1/2 teaspoon tarragon
- 1/2 teaspoon ground black pepper
- 1 teaspoon salt

**Directions**

1. In a cast-iron skillet, sweat the bell peppers together with the chopped pork sausages until the peppers are fragrant and the sausage begins to release liquid.

2. Lightly grease the inside of a baking dish with pan spray.

3. Throw all of the above ingredients into the prepared baking dish, including the sautéed mixture; stir to combine.

4. Bake at 345 degrees F approximately 9 minutes. Serve right away with the salad of choice.

# VEGETABLES

## 33. Bacon Asparagus Mix

Preparation time: 5 minutes

Cooking time: 8 minutes

Servings: 4

**Ingredients:**

- 1 pound asparagus spears, trimmed
- 2 tablespoons olive oil
- 2 garlic cloves, minced
- 1 teaspoon sweet paprika
- 3 tablespoons bacon, cooked and shredded
- A pinch of salt and black pepper

**Directions:**

1. In your air fryer's basket, combine the asparagus with the oil and the other ingredients except the bacon, toss and cook at 400 degrees F for 8 minutes.

2. Divide between plates and serve with the bacon sprinkled on top.

**Nutrition: calories 100, fat 2, fiber 5, carbs 8, protein 4**

## 34. Asparagus and Beets Mix

Preparation time: 4 minutes

Cooking time: 15 minutes

Servings: 4

**Ingredients:**

- 2 tablespoons olive oil
- 6 asparagus spears, trimmed and halved
- 2 beets, peeled and roughly cubed
- 2 tablespoons balsamic vinegar
- 1 teaspoon chili powder
- ½ tablespoon Cajun seasoning

**Directions:**

1. In your air fryer's basket, combine the beets with the asparagus and the other

ingredients, toss and cook at 390 degrees F for 15 minutes.

2. Divide the mix between plates and serve.

**Nutrition: calories 151, fat 3, fiber 4, carbs 9, protein 4**

## 35. Eggplant Salad

Preparation time: 10 minutes

Cooking time: 15 minutes

Servings: 4

**Ingredients:**

- 2 eggplants, peeled and roughly cubed
- 1 tablespoon olive oil
- 1 cup cherry tomatoes, halved
- 1 cup baby spinach
- 2 tablespoons balsamic vinegar
- Salt and black pepper to the taste
- 1 tablespoon cilantro, chopped

**Directions:**

1. In your air fryer's basket, combine the eggplants with the oil, tomatoes and the other ingredients, toss and cook at 390 degrees F for 15 minutes.

2. Divide everything between plates and serve.

**Nutrition: calories 151, fat 4, fiber 7, carbs 11, protein 8**

## 36. Parsley Squash Mix

Preparation time: 10 minutes

Cooking time: 20 minutes

Servings: 4

**Ingredients:**

- 1 pound butternut squash, roughly cubed
- 2 tablespoons olive oil
- 1 tablespoon lime juice
- 1 teaspoon cumin, ground
- Salt and black pepper to the taste
- • 1 tablespoon parsley, chopped

**Directions:**

1. In your air fryer, combine the squash with the oil, lime juice and the other ingredients, toss and cook at 380 degrees F for 20 minutes.

2. Divide everything between plates and serve.

**Nutrition: calories 200, fat 7, fiber 6, carbs 11, protein 7**

## 37. Orange Green Beans

Preparation time: 10 minutes

Cooking time: 15 minutes

Servings: 4

**Ingredients:**

- 2 pounds green beans, trimmed and halved
- Juice of 1 orange
- 2 teaspoons orange zest, grated
- 2 tablespoons olive oil
- A handful parsley, chopped
- 1 teaspoon chili powder

**Directions:**

1. In your air fryer, combine the green beans with the orange juice and the other ingredients, toss and cook at 350 degrees F for 15 minutes.

2. Divide everything between plates and serve.

**Nutrition: calories 151, fat 6, fiber 6, carbs 11, protein 5**

# SNACKS

## 38. Brussels Sprouts with Feta Cheese

Preparation Time: 20 minutes

Servings: 4

**Nutrition: 133 Calories; 8.2g Fat; 8.6g Carbs; 8.1g Protein; 3.2g Sugars; 3g Fiber**

**Ingredients**

- 3/4 pound Brussels sprouts, trimmed and cut off the ends
- 1 teaspoon kosher salt
- 1 tablespoon lemon zest
- Non-stick cooking spray
- 1 cup feta cheese, cubed

**Directions**

1. Firstly, peel the Brussels sprouts using a small paring knife. Toss the leaves with salt and lemon zest; spritz them with a cooking spray, coating all sides.

2. Bake at 380 degrees for 8 minutes; shake the cooking basket halfway through the cooking time and cook for 7 more minutes.

3. Make sure to work in batches so everything can cook evenly. Taste and adjust the seasonings. Serve with feta cheese. Bon appétit!

# 39. Saucy Chicken Wings with Sage

Preparation Time: 1 hour 10 minutes

Servings: 4

**Nutrition: 228 Calories; 6.5g Fat; 1.7g Carbs; 38.4g Protein; 1.1g Sugars; 0.3g Fiber**

**Ingredients**

- 1/3 cup almond flour
- 1/3 cup buttermilk
- 1 ½ pound chicken wings
- 1 tablespoon tamari sauce
- 1/3 teaspoon fresh sage
- 1 teaspoon mustard seeds
- 1/2 teaspoon garlic paste
- 1/2 teaspoon freshly ground mixed peppercorns
- 1/2 teaspoon seasoned salt
- 2 teaspoons fresh basil

**Directions**

1. Place the seasonings along with the garlic paste, chicken wings, buttermilk, and tamari sauce in a large-sized mixing dish. Let it soak about 55 minutes; drain the wings.

2. Dredge the wings in the almond flour and transfer them to the Air Fryer cooking basket.

3. Air-fry for 16 minutes at 355 degrees F. Serve on a nice serving platter with a dressing on the side. Bon appétit!

## 40. Crispy Crackling Bites

Preparation Time: 50 minutes

Servings: 10

**Nutrition: 245 Calories; 14.1g Fat; 0g Carbs; 27.6g Protein; 0g Sugars; 0.5g Fiber**

**Ingredients**

- 1 pound pork rind raw, scored by the butcher
- 1 tablespoon sea salt
- 2 tablespoons smoked paprika

**Directions**

1. Sprinkle and rub salt on the skin side of the pork rind. Allow it to sit for 30 minutes.

2. Roast at 380 degrees F for 8 minutes; turn them over and cook for a further 8 minutes or until blistered.

3. Sprinkle the smoked paprika all over the pork crackling and serve. Bon appétit!

## 41. Roasted Spicy Hot Dogs

Preparation Time: 20 minutes

Servings: 6

**Nutrition: 542 Calories; 47.2g Fat; 5.7g Carbs; 21.1g Protein; 3.6g Sugars; 0.2g Fiber**

**Ingredients**

- 6 hot dogs
- 1 tablespoon mustard
- 6 tablespoons ketchup, no sugar added

**Directions**

1. Place the hot dogs in the lightly greased Air Fryer basket.

2. Bake at 380 degrees F for 15 minutes, turning them over halfway through the cooking time to promote even cooking.

3. Serve on cocktail sticks with the mustard and ketchup. Enjoy!

# 42. Celery Chips with Harissa Mayonnaise Sauce

Preparation Time: 30 minutes

Servings: 3

**Nutrition: 234 Calories; 23.7g Fat; 4.3g Carbs; 1.3g Protein; 1.9g Sugars; 1.5g Fiber**

**Ingredients**

- 1/2 pound celery root
- 2 tablespoons olive oil
- Sea salt and ground black pepper, to taste
- Harissa Mayo
- 1/4 cup mayonnaise
- 2 tablespoons sour cream
- 1/2 tablespoon harissa paste
- • 1/4 teaspoon ground cumin
- Salt, to taste

**Directions**

1. Cut the celery root into desired size and shape.

2. Then, preheat your Air Fryer to 400 degrees F. Now, spritz the Air Fryer basket with cooking spray.

3. Toss the celery chips with the olive oil, salt, and black pepper. Bake in the preheated Air Fryer for 25 to 30 minutes, turning them over every 10 minutes to promote even cooking.

4. Meanwhile, mix all ingredients for the harissa mayo. Place in your refrigerator until ready to serve. Bon appétit!

# DESSERT

## 43. Pineapple Cake

Preparation time: 10 minutes

Cooking time: 35 minutes

Servings: 6

**Ingredients:**

- 2 cups almond flour
- ½ teaspoon baking soda
- ½ teaspoon vanilla extract
- 2 eggs, whisked
- 1 pineapple, peeled and cubed
- 3 tablespoons sugar
- ¼ cup almond milk
- 4 tablespoons vegetable oil
- Cooking spray

**Directions:**

1. In a bowl, combine the flour with the baking soda, vanilla and the other ingredients except the cooking spray and whisk well.

2. Pour this into a cake pan that fits your air fryer greased with the cooking spray, transfer to your air fryer, cook on 320 degrees F for 35 minutes, cool down, cut and serve it.

**Nutrition: calories 200, fat 6, fiber 7, carbs 12, protein 4**

## 44. Cream Cheese Ramekins

Preparation time: 10 minutes

Cooking time: 20 minutes

Servings: 4

**Ingredients:**

- 2 tablespoons butter, melted
- 2 cups cream cheese, soft
- 2 eggs, whisked
- ½ cup sugar
- ½ teaspoon vanilla extract

**Directions:**

1. In a bowl, combine the cream cheese with the eggs and the other ingredients, whisk well, divide into 4 ramekins, introduce them in your air fryer's basket and cook at 340 degrees F for 20 minutes.

2. Serve cold.

**Nutrition: calories 212, fat 12, fiber 6, carbs 12, protein 7**

## 45. Berries Cream

Preparation time: 10 minutes

Cooking time: 15 minutes

Servings: 4

**Ingredients:**

- 2 cups blackberries
- 2 tablespoons lemon zest, grated
- ½ tablespoon lemon juice
- ¼ teaspoon sugar
- 2 cups heavy cream

**Directions:**

1. In a bowl, combine the berries with the lemon zest and the other ingredients, whisk well, divide into 4 ramekins, introduce them in your air fryer and cook at 330 degrees F for 15 minutes.

2. Serve the cream really cold.

**Nutrition: calories 202, fat 8, fiber 2, carbs 6, protein 7**

## 46. Caramel Cream

Preparation time: 10 minutes

Cooking time: 15 minutes

Servings: 6

**Ingredients:**

- 2 tablespoons butter, melted
- 8 ounces heavy cream
- 4 eggs
- 3 tablespoons sugar
- 1 tablespoon caramel syrup

**Directions:**

1. In a bowl, combine the butter with the caramel and the other ingredients, whisk well divide into 6 ramekins, introduce them in the fryer and cook at 320 degrees F for 15 minutes.

2. Leave aside to cool down and serve.

**Nutrition: calories 234, fat 13, fiber 4, carbs 11, protein 5 **

## 47. Apricot Crumble

Preparation Time: 15 minutes

Cooking time: 20 minutes

Servings: 2

**Ingredients:**

- ¼ cup fresh apricot
- 1 tablespoon brown sugar
- 1 tablespoon butter
- ½ teaspoon ground cinnamon
- 3 tablespoon flour
- 1 teaspoon lime juice

**Directions:**

1. Halve the apricots and then remove the stones.

2. Then chop the apricots and sprinkle with the ½ tablespoon of sugar.

3. Sprinkle the apricots with the lemon juice.

4. Mix the mixture.

5. Then combine together butter, remaining brown sugar, ground cinnamon, and flour.

6. Knead the dough.

7. Then crumble the dough with the help of the fingertips.

8. Put the apricot mixture into the cake tin and spread it well.

9. Then sprinkle the apricots with the crumbled dough.

10. Press it gently.

11. Preheat the air fryer to 360 F.

12. Put the cake tin in the air fryer and cook for 20 minutes.

13. When the meal is cooked – let it chill briefly.

14. Enjoy!

**Nutrition: calories 121, fat 6, fiber 1, carbs 16, protein 1.6**

## 48. Cinnamon Doughnuts

Preparation Time: 15 minutes

Cooking time: 15 minutes

Servings: 2

**Ingredients:**

- 1 teaspoon sugar
- 1 teaspoon butter
- 1/3 cup flour
- ¼ teaspoon salt
- 1 egg yolk
- 3 tablespoon sour cream
- 1 teaspoon ground cinnamon
- 1 tablespoon brown sugar

**Directions:**

1. Combine together brown sugar, butter, flour, salt, and sour cream.

2. Knead the smooth and non-sticky dough.

3. Then roll the dough using the rolling pin.

4. After this, use the cutter to make the medium doughnuts.

5. Whisk the egg yolk.

6. Preheat the air fryer to 360 F.

7. Brush the doughnuts with the whisked egg and put in the air fryer.

8. Cook the doughnuts for 15 minutes.

9. When the surface of the doughnuts is light brown – flip them to another side.

10. Meanwhile, combine together sugar with the cinnamon.

11. When the doughnuts are cooked – sprinkle them gently with the sugar-cinnamon mixture.

12. Serve the doughnuts immediately.

13. Enjoy!

**Nutrition: calories 186, fat 8.2, fiber 1.2, carbs 24.3, protein 4.2**

## 49. Raisin Muffins

Preparation Time: 15 minutes

Cooking time: 10 minutes

Servings: 2

**Ingredients:**

- 1 oz raisins
- ¼ cup flour
- 2 tablespoon butter
- ¼ teaspoon baking soda
- 1 tablespoon brown sugar
- 1 egg
- ½ teaspoon vanilla extract
- 1 teaspoon apple cider vinegar

**Directions:**

1. Preheat the air fryer to 360 F.

2. Combine together flour, baking soda, and brown sugar.

3. Then add raisins, butter, vanilla extract, and apple cider vinegar.

4. Crack the egg into the mixture.

5. Take the fork and mix the mixture well.

6. Then use the hand mixer to make the homogenous mass. The dough should be liquid as a batter.

7. Pour the muffin dough into the muffin molds.

8. Place the muffin molds in the air fryer basket.

9. Cook the muffins for 10 minutes or until the top of the muffins are light brown.

10. When the raisin muffins are cooked – let them chill little.

11. Then discard the muffins from the muffin molds, if you use the silicone molds.

12. Enjoy!

**Nutrition: calories 253, fat 13.9, fiber 0.9, carbs 27.9, protein 5**

## 50. Chocolate Muffins

Preparation Time: 15 minutes

Cooking time: 10 minutes

Servings: 2

**Ingredients:**

- 2 oz chocolate chips
- 2 oz butter
- 1 egg
- 1 teaspoon vanilla extract
- 1 teaspoon sour cream
- 1 teaspoon cocoa powder
- 1/3 cup flour
- 1 tablespoon sugar
- 1 teaspoon lemon juice

**Directions:**

1. Make the butter soft and combine it with the vanilla extract and sour cream.

2. Add cocoa powder, flour, sugar, and lemon juice.

3. After this beat the egg in the flour mixture and mix it with the help of the hand mixer until homogenous.

4. Sprinkle the dough with the chocolate chips and stir it carefully.

5. Preheat the air fryer to 365 F.

6. Use the spoon to fill the muffin molds with the dough.

7. Put the muffin molds in the air fryer basket.

8. Cook the muffins for 10 minutes.

9. Then check if the muffins are cooked using the toothpick.

10. Chill the muffins till the room temperature.

11. Serve the dessert!

**Nutrition: calories 498, fat 34.4, fiber 1.8, carbs 39.8, protein 7.6**

# CONCLUSION

I hope this Air Fryer Cookbook helps you understand the dynamics and principles of this revolutionary

kitchen appliance, why you should use it and how it's going to change your outlook on food preparation and healthy living.

The next step is to get into the right frame of mind and decide that it's time to take charge of your eating habits by only putting the best organic and free range ingredients in your Air Fryer.

Even if you have never tried the Air Fryer before, I can promise you one thing, after the 30 days, you will be kicking yourself for having not discovered this sooner.I hope it was able to inspire you to clean up your kitchen from all the useless appliances that clutter your countertop and start putting the Air Fryer to good use.

The Air Fryer is definitely a change in lifestyle that will make things much easier for you and your family. You'll discover increased energy, decreased hunger, a boosted metabolism and of course a LOT more free time!

I encourage you to share these recipes with family and friends, tell them about this book, and let them know that the Instant Pot can be the best investment that one can make.

It'd be greatly appreciated! Happy Air Frying!

CPSIA information can be obtained
at www.ICGtesting.com
Printed in the USA
LVHW021320230121
677173LV00005B/667